SAMUEL BARBER
MUSIC FOR VIOLIN AND PIANO

Edited by Richard Walters

Selected Violin Parts Edited by Frank Almond

ED 4473
First Printing: November 2010

ISBN 978-1-4234-7538-5

G. SCHIRMER, Inc.

DISTRIBUTED BY

HAL•LEONARD®
CORPORATION

7777 W. BLUEMOUND RD. P.O. BOX 13819 MILWAUKEE, WI 53213

www.schirmer.com
www.halleonard.com

SAMUEL BARBER
MUSIC FOR VIOLIN AND PIANO

Edited by Richard Walters

Selected Violin Parts Edited by Frank Almond

ED 4473
First Printing: November 2010

ISBN 978-1-4234-7538-5

G. SCHIRMER, *Inc.*

DISTRIBUTED BY

HAL•LEONARD®
CORPORATION
7777 W. BLUEMOUND RD. P.O. BOX 13819 MILWAUKEE, WI 53213

www.schirmer.com
www.halleonard.com

Samuel Barber in his studio at the American Academy in Rome, 1953

CONTENTS

Recording Artists on the CDs:
Frank Almond, violin
[1] Laura Ward, piano
[2] Michael Mizrahi, piano
[3] Elena Abend, piano

Recorded by Remote Planet Recording, Ric Probst, engineer, Milwaukee, Wisconsin.
Tracks 1, 13 recorded September, 2010. Tracks 2-5, 7-12, 14 recorded February, 2010. Track 6 recorded March, 2006.

ABOUT THE MUSIC

Allegro agitato
third movement from Sonata for Violin and Piano in F minor

This movement appears here in a first edition, previously unpublished. The companion CD also marks the first recording released of this music. Manuscript source: Library of Congress. There are two versions of the violin part presented in this edition. Barber included very few indications for bowing in the manuscript. The first version of the violin part is unedited in this regard. A second version of the violin part, edited by Frank Almond, makes editorial bowing suggestions.

The sonata was composed during 1928, begun in the winter, with work continuing in Europe in the summer. Barber completed the three movement sonata on November 8, 1928. A program dated December 10, 1928 from the Curtis Institute of Music is record of the first performance, played by Gama Gilbert, violin, and the composer at the piano. Gama Gilbert was a classmate of Barber's at Curtis and remained a close friend and champion of the composer's music, and was the catalyst some years later for the commission that led to the violin concerto. Gilbert died at a young age in 1940.

The violin part only of an early version of the first movement was discovered in 2005 in the estate of Gama Gilbert's widow. The manuscript is reproduced in this edition in Appendix 1. The violin/piano score of this movement has not been located. The second movement is lost. A holograph of the third movement was discovered in 2006 in the estate of Thomas Bostelle, an artist who boarded for a time at the Barber family home in West Chester, Pennsylvania. Barber scholar Barbara Heyman speculates that Bostelle may have received the manuscript from Barber's mother. The surviving material of the sonata was subsequently donated to the Library of Congress.

The sonata won the Joseph H. Bearns Prize in Music in 1929, a prize established in 1921 to encourage talented American composers aged 25 or younger. (Barber again won the same prize in 1933 for the *Overture to School for Scandal*.) Even so, Barber eventually regarded the violin sonata as student work and did not seek its publication. The chamber music coach at Curtis, Louis Bailly, reportedly told Barber that the sonata was reminiscent of Brahms, a composer Barber greatly admired. Nevertheless, the comment annoyed Barber, who apparently felt as if he was perceived as being in the great composer's shadow and "consigned to invisibility." This may have colored his opinion of the sonata thereafter. The Sonata for Cello and Piano, which shares some kinship in style with the Sonata for Violin and Piano, was composed four years later.

Canzonetta

Canzonetta was originally scored for solo oboe and string orchestra, Op. 48 (posthumous). Barber was commissioned by the New York Philharmonic to compose an oboe concerto for the farewell performance of Harold Gomberg, principal with the orchestra 1943-1977. Composition began in the summer of 1978. Barber was in poor health, and in the autumn of that year was diagnosed with multiple myeloma. He began by writing what was intended to be the second movement of the oboe concerto. Two short score versions of this movement were composed. By 1980 Barber's health had declined and he knew that he would not have the strength or life left to finish the concerto. Believing the movement could stand alone, he gave it the title *Canzonetta*. Paul Witke, the composer's longtime editor at G. Schirmer, asked Charles Turner, Barber's only composition student ever and a close personal friend since the 1950s, to orchestrate the short score, which included Barber's indications about instrumentation. In the oboe and piano reduction edition that was ultimately published Turner wrote the following brief introduction:

> "I like to give my best themes to the oboe," said Sam Barber. This *Canzonetta* for oboe and strings was meant to be the slow movement of an oboe concerto commissioned by the New York Philharmonic, but soon after Sam began it in 1978, his doctor told him he had cancer. The other two movements were never written—nor was anything else—before he died in 1981. In this *Canzonetta* we find the form of Sam's life imitating that of his art by making a simple final statement and farewell.

The original version of *Canzonetta*, for oboe and string orchestra, was first performed December 17, 1981, by Harold Gomberg, oboe, and the New York Philharmonic, conducted by Zubin Mehta.

An arrangement for violin and piano, created for this collection, seemed a natural idea, considering the nature of the music. The violin part is primarily but not entirely a direct transcription of the original oboe solo line. For idiomatic reasons in creating a violin and piano piece, in some stretches the violin solo line is an adaptation of the violin part in the string orchestra. Such an approach is used in measures 44-55, 77-84, and 89-102. Measures 111-113 are from a solo violin line in the orchestration. Other idiomatic adjustments were made for the violin. The violin part was edited by Frank Almond. The piano part is principally taken from the piano reduction by William Holab, published in the edition for oboe and piano, with adaptations.

Hermit Songs Suite

Hermit Songs, a cycle of ten songs for voice and piano, was composed from November 1952 to February 1953. It is one of the most significant and beloved of American song cycles. Barber was unquestionably a master of art song, one of the major twentieth century composers of the genre. The texts for the cycle are English translations of medieval Gaelic poems. The first performance was by soprano Leontyne Price and Barber on October 30, 1953, at the Library of Congress, Washington, D.C. Price and Barber recorded the cycle in 1954.

The transcriptions for violin were created for this collection, and first recorded for the companion CD. The violin parts were edited by Frank Almond. The piano parts are unaltered from Barber's original compositions. Barber used no time signatures in the original song cycle; they have been added in these transcriptions.

St. Ita's Vision

The song was composed on January 9, 1953. The eighth century words, originally in Gaelic, are attributed to Saint Ita, translated into English by Chester Kallman. Ita is pronounced Eeta. The song text appears below. The initial recitative/introduction is omitted in the violin/piano transcription, which begins with the words "Infant Jesus." A brief piano introduction was created for the transcription by repeating the first piano measure.

"I will take nothing from my Lord," said she,
"unless He gives me His Son from Heaven
In the form of a Baby that I may nurse Him."
So that Christ came down to her in the form of a Baby
and then she said:

"Infant Jesus, at my breast,
Nothing in this world is true
Save, O tiny nursling, You.
Infant Jesus, at my breast,
By my heart ev'ry night,
You I nurse are not
A churl but were begot
On Mary the Jewess by Heaven's Light.
Infant Jesus, at my breast,
what King is there but You who could
Give everlasting Good?
wherefor I give my food.
Sing to Him, maidens, sing your best!
There is none that has such right
To your song as Heaven's King
Who ev'ry night
Is Infant Jesus at my breast."

The Monk and His Cat

The song was composed on February 16, 1953, and dedicated to Isabelle Vengerova, a gift for her seventy-sixth birthday. Vengerova was Barber's piano teacher at Curtis. Other Vengerova piano students over the years included Leonard Bernstein, Lukas Foss, Leonard Pennario, Gary Graffm and Abbey Simon. The words to the song are anonymous eighth or ninth century Gaelic, translated into English by W.H. Auden. The song text appears below.

Pangur, white Pangur,
How happy we are
Alone together,
Scholar and cat.
Each has his own work to do daily;
For you it is hunting, for me study.
Your shining eye watches the wall;
my feeble eye is fixed on a book.
You rejoice when your claws
Entrap a mouse;
I rejoice when my mind
Fathoms a problem.
Pleased with his own art,
Neither hinders the other;
Thus we live ever
Without tedium and envy.

The Desire for Hermitage

The song, the last of the cycle, was composed on January 15, 1953. The words are anonymous eighth or ninth century Gaelic, translated by Sean O'Faolain and altered by the composer. The song text appears below.

Ah! To be all alone in a little cell with nobody near me;
beloved that pilgrimage before the last pilgrimage to Death.
Singing the passing hours to cloudy Heaven;
feeding upon dry bread and water from the cold spring.
That will be an end to evil when I am alone
in a lovely little corner among tombs
far from the houses of the great.
Ah! to be all alone in a little cell,
alone I came into the world,
alone I shall go from it.

Canzone

The piece began as *Elegy* for flute and piano, composed in 1959. Barber retitled *Elegy* as *Canzone* in 1961, and made a version for violin and piano. Barber recomposed it, adding further material and orchestration, for the second movement of the Piano Concerto.

The related composition, the Piano Concerto, Op. 38, was commissioned by G. Schirmer to celebrate the centennial anniversary of the founding of the New York publishing house. The concerto was also designated to have its prominent premiere in the week of inaugural concerts at the opening of Philharmonic Hall (later renamed Avery Fisher Hall) at the new Lincoln Center in New York City. Composition was completed on September 9, 1962. It was first performed on September 24, 1962, by John Browning, piano, with the Boston Symphony Orchestra, conducted by Erich Leinsdorf.

Suite from Souvenirs

Souvenirs, a six movement suite, was originally composed in 1952 for piano, four hands. Barber wrote it to play with his friend Charles Turner, who had encouraged the composer to write something similar in spirit to two-piano arrangements of lighter music they had heard together at the Blue Angel Club. Barber made the solo piano version in 1952. A two-piano version followed in the same year. The composer worked on the orchestrated version in 1952. The orchestral suite was premiered by Chicago Symphony Orchestra on November 12, 1953, conducted by Fritz Reiner. *Souvenirs* as a ballet score was premiered on November 15, 1955 by New York City Ballet, choreographed by Todd Bolender.

Barber commented: "In 1952 I was writing some duets for one piano to play with a friend, and Lincoln Kirstein suggested I orchestrate them for a ballet. Commissioned by Ballet Society, the suite consists of a waltz, schottische, pas de deux, two-step, hesitation tango, and gallop. One might imagine a divertissement in a setting of the Palm Court of the Hotel Plaza in New York, the year about 1914, epoch of the first tangos; 'Souvenirs' remembered with affection, not in irony or with tongue in cheek, but in amused tenderness."

The transcriptions for violin and piano were created for this collection, and first recorded for the companion CD. Sources for the transcriptions included all Barber's versions, including the orchestrated score. The violin parts were edited by Frank Almond.

Waltz
Pas de deux
Hesitation-Tango

Three Song Transcriptions

A master of art song composition, Barber composed well over 70 songs during his lifetime. They are among his first compositions, and were his first published works. The transcriptions for violin were created for this collection, and first recorded for the companion CD. Except for transpositions, the piano parts are unaltered from the Barber's original compositions. The violin parts were edited by Frank Almond.

Lament

The original song title is "With rue my heart is laden," a setting of a text by A.E. Housman, published in *A Shropshire Lad*, 1896. It was composed when Barber was seventeen, on June 30, 1927. This is one of three songs that were Barber's first published opus, published in 1936. The song text appears below.

With rue my heart is laden
For golden friends I had,
For many a rose-lipt maiden
And many a lightfoot lad.
By brooks too broad for leaping
The lightfoot boys are laid;
The rose-lipt girls are sleeping
In fields where roses fade.

The Secrets of the Old

Composition of the song was completed in September, 1938, a setting of a text by William Butler Yeats from a set of poems, *A Man Young and Old*. It was included in Four Songs, Op. 13, published in 1941. The song text appears below.

I have old women's secrets now
That had those of the young;
Madge tells me what I dared not think
When my blood was strong,
And what had drowned a lover once
Sounds like an old song.
Though Margery is stricken dumb
If thrown in Madge's way,
We three make up a solitude;
For none alive today
Can known the stories that we know
Or say the things we say:
How such a man pleased women most
Of all that are gone,
How such a pair loved many years
And such a pair but one,
Stories of the bed of straw
Or the bed of down.

Sure on this shining night

Composition of the song was completed in September, 1938, a setting of a text by James Agee, from the 1934 collection *Permit Me Voyage*. It was included in Four Songs, Op. 13, published in 1941. One of the most famous of Barber's art songs, the composer later created a voice and orchestra version, as well as a choral arrangement. Barber told an anecdote about a 1979 conversation with a New York City telephone operator who asked him to sing the beginning of "Sure on this shining night" to prove that he was indeed Samuel Barber. The song text appears below.

Sure on this shining night
Of starmade shadows round,
Kindness must watch for me
This side the ground.
The late year lies down the north.
All is healed, all is health.
High summer holds the earth.
Hearts all whole.
Sure on this shining night
I weep for wonder wand'ring far alone
Of shadows on the stars.

Gypsy Dance

This composition appears here in a first edition, previously unpublished. The companion CD also marks the first recording released of this music. Manuscript source: Library of Congress.

The manuscript is dated October 17, 1922. Written at age twelve, it was Barber's first instrumental work. The music originated in an unfinished opera, *The Rose Tree*, composed at age ten to a libretto by the Barber family's Irish cook. Studying the manuscripts for piano and voice of *The Rose Tree*, it appears that *Gypsy Dance* for violin and piano had only scant basis, though Barber's manuscript states "Arranged for a Violin Solo." The cover of the manuscript, design by Barber's friend William Palmer Lear (who shared the composer's exact birth date), and the first page of music appear in Appendix 2.

Adagio

The famous "Adagio," one of the most recorded pieces of twentieth century music, originated as the second movement of String Quartet in B minor, Op. 11. Composition of this movement was completed in St. Wolfgang, Austria, on September 19, 1936. In a letter to a friend Barber wrote, "I have just finished the slow movement of my quartet today, and it is a knockout!" The quartet was first performed by the Pro Arte String Quartet on December 14, 1936, at the American Academy, Rome, Italy. The movement gained its fame when in 1938 Barber made the adaptation of the Adagio for string orchestra (Adagio for Strings) for Arturo Toscanini, who first conducted it on a landmark NBC radio broadcast of November 5, 1938. On the same program Toscanini also conducted the premiere of Barber's Essay (No. 1) for Orchestra, Op. 12. Toscanini, the most powerful and well-regarded conductor of the era, had previously avoided American compositions almost entirely. His endorsement and performance of Barber's music made a great impact, and spurred a controversial debate in letters by various writers published in *The New York Times* about the state of American music and whether Barber's music fairly represented it. There was no doubt, however, about the lasting appeal of the Adagio, which has been well-known since then. Barber later made an adaptation of the Adagio for chorus, and approved other arrangements. This transcription for violin and piano was first published in 1996.

Richard Walters
Editor

Principal Sources Consulted

Heyman, Barbara B. *Samuel Barber: A Thematic Catalogue of the Complete Works*. Oxford University Press, Forthcoming.
Heyman, Barbara B. *Samuel Barber: The Composer and His Music*. New York, Oxford: Oxford University Press, 1992.
Wentzel, Wayne C. *Samuel Barber: A Guide to Research*. New York, London. Routledge Music Bibliographies, 2001.
Dickinson, Peter (editor). *Samuel Barber Remembered: A Centenary Tribute*. Rochester. University of Rochester Press, 2010.

PREFACE

Notice to Mother and nobody else

Dear Mother: I have written this to tell you my worrying secret.
Now don't cry when you read it because it is neither yours nor my
fault. I suppose I will have to tell it now without any nonsense. To begin
with I was not meant to be an athlet [sic]. I was meant to be a composer,
and will be I'm sure. I'll ask you one more thing—Don't ask me to try
to forget this unpleasant thing and go play football.—Please—Sometimes
I've been worrying about this so much that it makes me mad (not very),

> Love,
> Sam Barber II
> [written at age 9]

Few people are as self-aware of personal destiny at such a young age as was Sam Barber. Even at 9-years-old he knew that he was a composer, and was at least somewhat aware of the insecurities and consequences of an unconventional, creative life.

Born on March 9, 1910 to Dr. Roy Barber and his wife, Daisy, Samuel Osborne Barber II (named after his paternal grandfather) grew up in West Chester, Pennsylvania, 30 miles from Philadelphia. Sam's father had expectations his son would not fulfill. The composer stated, "I was supposed to be a doctor. I was supposed to go to Princeton. And everything I was supposed to do I didn't." Though he played piano from an early age (undoubtedly helped by his pianist mother), and began composing at age 7, music lessons did not begin until age 9, when he started formally studying piano. At 14 Barber entered the Curtis Institute of Music, a member of the first class to attend the newly formed school. He studied composition, piano and voice there. His composition and theory teacher, Rosario Scalero, was a far-reaching influence. With Scalero for nine years, Barber studied in a very thorough, traditional European approach.

Barber most significant musical inspirations from a young age well into adulthood were his aunt, Louise Homer, a professional singer at the Metropolitan Opera, and her husband and Barber's uncle, Sidney Homer, a respectable composer. Both were encouraging mentors and supporters.

Barber composed few works for violin. Besides the Concerto for Violin and Orchestra, he only wrote three pieces for violin. Two of the three are published and recorded for the first time in this collection: *Gypsy Dance*, written at age 12, and *Allegro agitato*, the recently discovered third movement of a violin sonata composed at age 18. His only other violin work was *Canzone*, an arrangement the composer made of a piece originally written for flute and piano.

Considering the lack of available Barber violin music, transcriptions were a likely avenue. There are further reasons beyond the practical for pursuing new transcriptions for this collection. Barber's timelessly appealing music is inherently lyrical, and it was not a far stretch of the imagination to find suitable selections that are well-suited to the instrument. We hope that the transcriptions included here prove the point.

I would like to thank Frank Almond for his invaluable suggestions and advice for the violin parts for the newly published pieces, as well as for all the new transcriptions created for this collection. I also extend my thanks to David Flachs, Barbara Heyman, Laura Ward, Elena Abend, Michael Mizrahi, our recording engineer Ric Probst, the always responsive and helpful staff at the Library of Congress, and assistant editor Joshua Parman.

> Richard Walters
> Editor

CONTENTS

Recording Artists on the CDs:
Frank Almond, violin
[1] Laura Ward, piano
[2] Michael Mizrahi, piano
[3] Elena Abend, piano

Recorded by Remote Planet Recording, Ric Probst, engineer, Milwaukee, Wisconsin.
Tracks 1, 13 recorded September, 2010. Tracks 2-5, 7-12, 14 recorded February, 2010. Track 6 recorded March, 2006.

Allegro agitato

third movement from Sonata for Violin and Piano in F minor

unedited bowing★

Samuel Barber
1928

★ Barber indicated very few such markings. See page 10 for an edited version of the violin part.

6

Allegro agitato
third movement from Sonata for Violin and Piano in F minor
with editorial bowing suggestions

Samuel Barber
1928

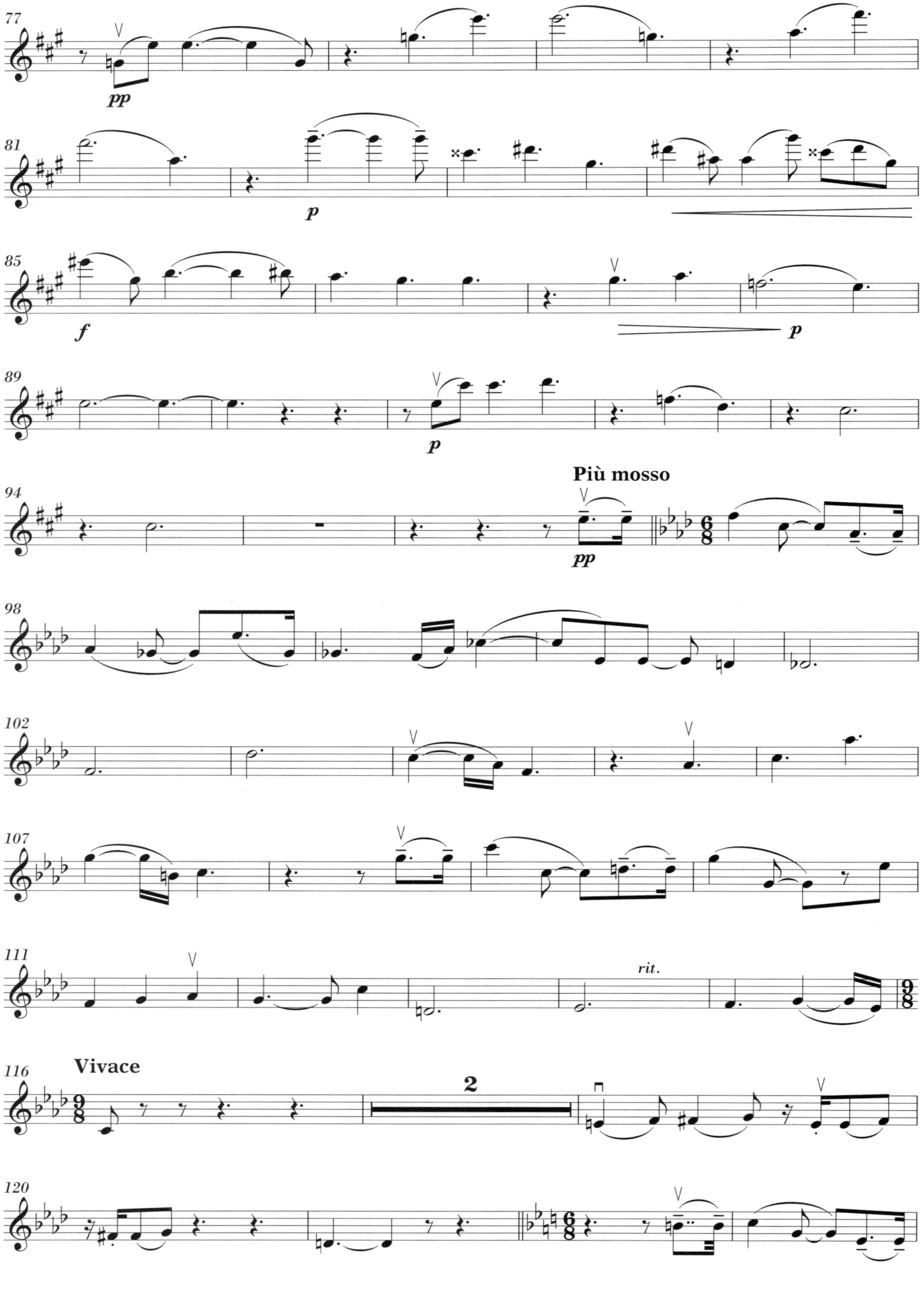
Più mosso
rit.
Vivace

Hermit Songs Suite
St. Ita's Vision

Transcribed by Richard Walters

Samuel Barber

The Monk and His Cat

Transcribed by Richard Walters

Samuel Barber

* Barber wrote this footnote in the original song publication: "Notes marked (–) in these two measures should be slightly longer, pochissimo rubato..."

The Desire for Hermitage

Transcribed by Richard Walters

Samuel Barber

Canzonetta

Transcribed by Richard Walters

Samuel Barber

20

Canzone

Transcribed by the Composer

Samuel Barber

Three Song Transcriptions
Lament

Transcribed by Richard Walters

Samuel Barber

Andante cantabile ♩ = 84

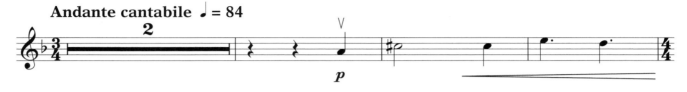

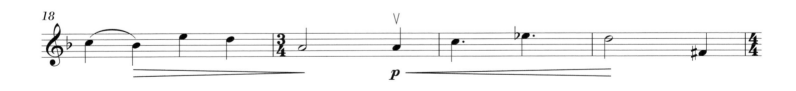

The Secrets of the Old

Transcribed by Richard Walters

Samuel Barber

Sure on this shining night

Transcribed by Richard Walters

Samuel Barber

Suite from Souvenirs
Waltz

Transcribed by Joshua Parman

Samuel Barber

Pas de deux

Transcribed by Joshua Parman

Samuel Barber

Hesitation-Tango

Transcribed by Joshua Parman

Samuel Barber

Gypsy Dance

Samuel Barber
1922

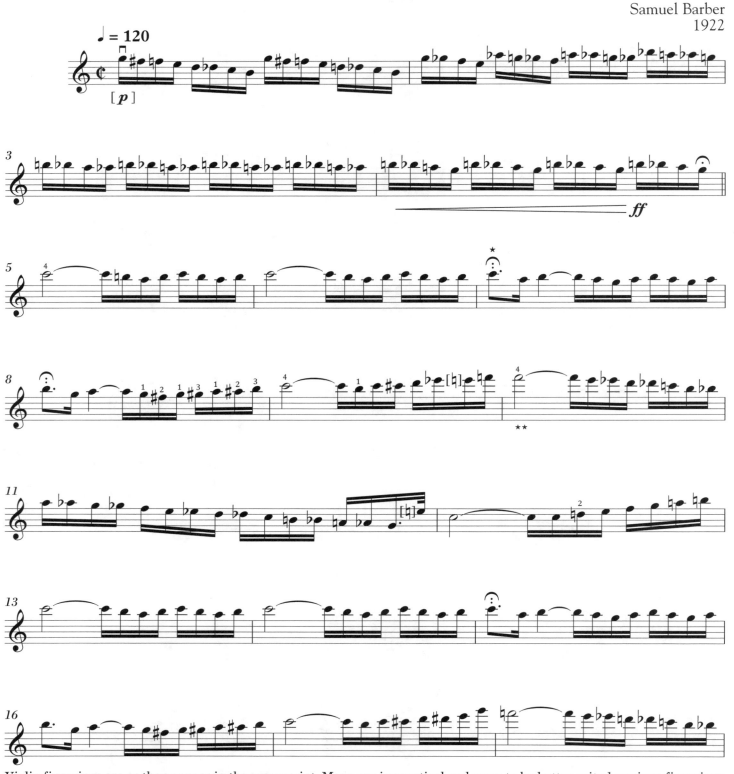

Violin fingerings are as they appear in the manuscript. Many are impractical and seem to be better suited as piano fingerings. All bowing and phrasing indications are editorial suggestions.

 A possible realization of Barber's intentions. See also mm. 8, 15, and 33.

** Barber wrote *"cadenza"* under measure 7 in the violin part.

Adagio

Transcribed by Jerry Lanning

Samuel Barber

Molto adagio

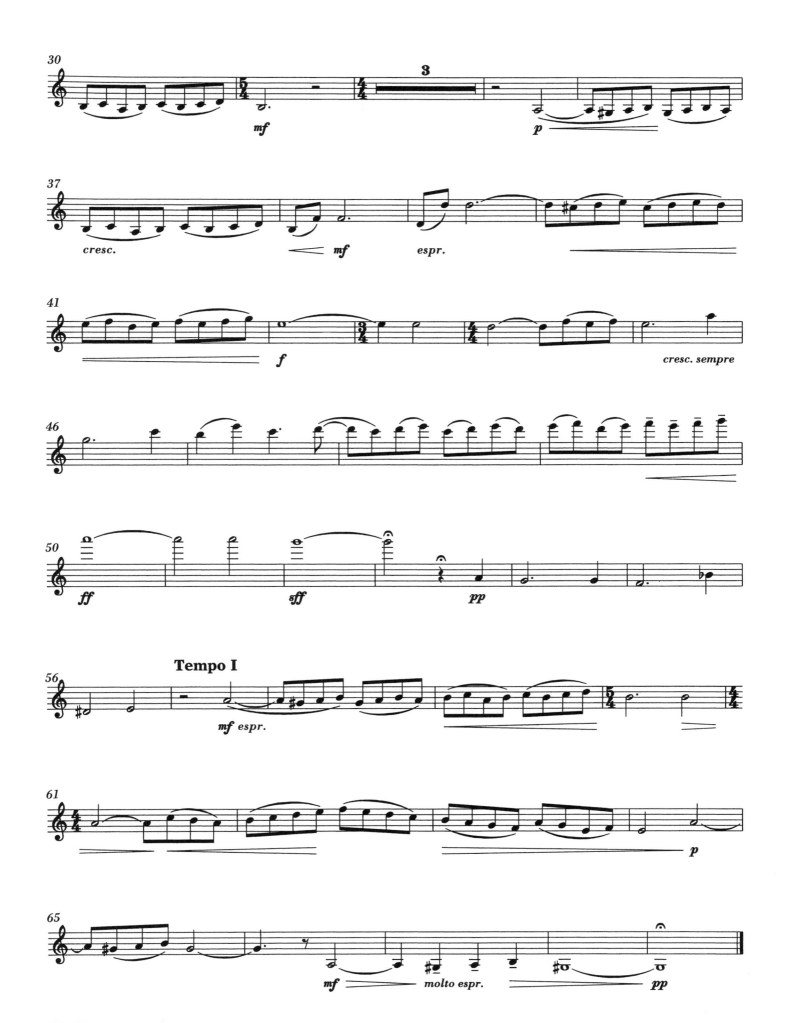

The Monk and His Cat

Transcribed by Richard Walters

Samuel Barber

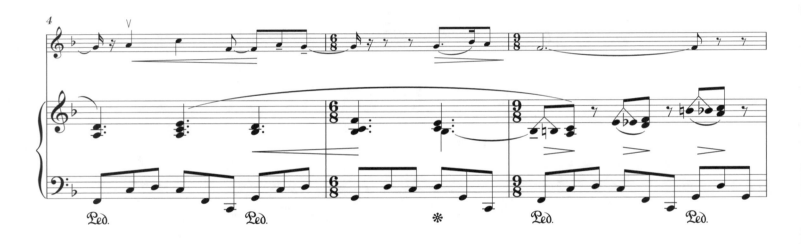

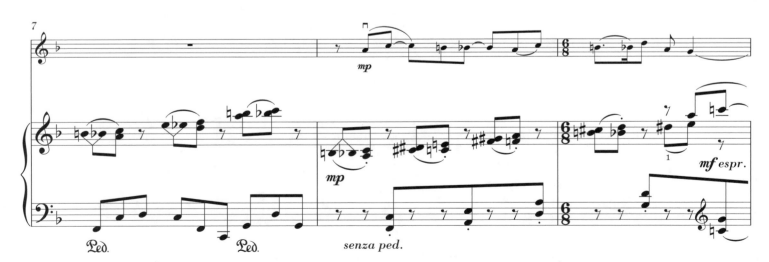

* Barber wrote this footnote in the original song publication: "Notes marked (–) in these two measures should be slightly longer, pochissimo rubato; also on the fourth page." The piano fingerings are Barber's.

The Desire for Hermitage

Transcribed by Richard Walters

Samuel Barber

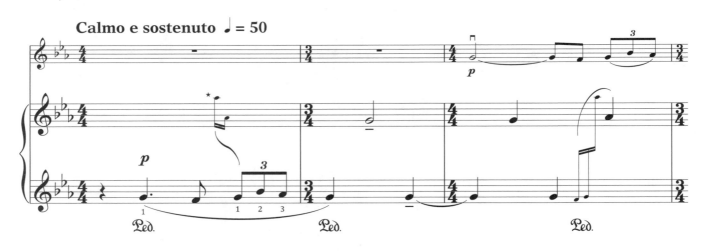

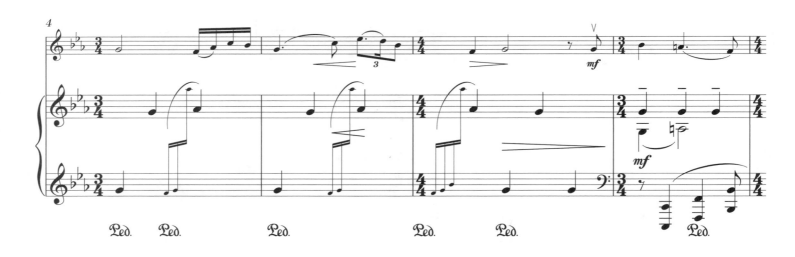

* Barber's footnote in the original published song: "All grace-notes somewhat longer, rubato."

Canzone

Transcribed by the Composer

Samuel Barber

Suite from Souvenirs
Waltz

Transcribed by Joshua Parman

Samuel Barber

Tempo di valtzer, allegro con brio ♩. = **72**

52

54

58

Pas de deux

Transcribed by Joshua Parman

Samuel Barber

Hesitation-Tango

Transcribed by Joshua Parman

Samuel Barber

Pochissimo più mosso, sempre in 2

sempre in 2

Three Song Transcriptions
Lament

Transcribed by Richard Walters

Samuel Barber

Andante cantabile ♩ = 84

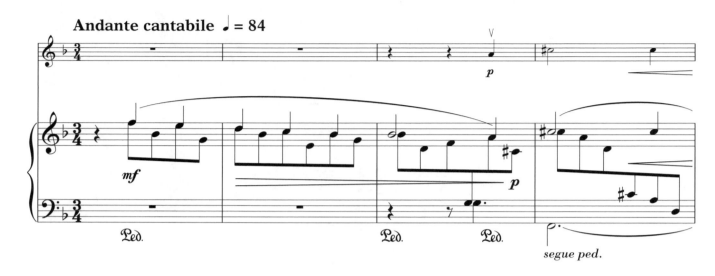

The Secrets of the Old

Transcribed by Richard Walters

Samuel Barber

Samuel Barber in his studio at the American Academy in Rome, 1953

Sure on this shining night

Transcribed by Richard Walters

Samuel Barber

Adagio

Samuel Barber

Transcribed by Jerry Lanning

Molto adagio

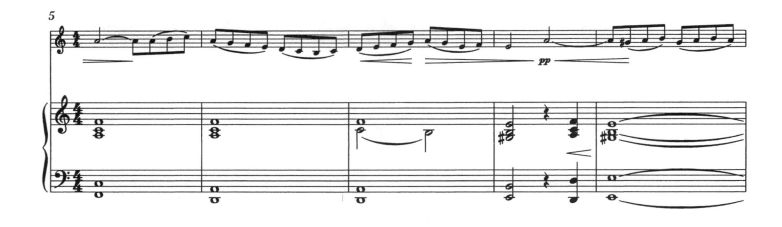

Gypsy Dance

Samuel Barber
1922

Violin fingerings are as they appear in the manuscript. Many are impractical and seem to be better suited as piano fingerings. All bowing and phrasing indications are editorial suggestions.

A possible realization of Barber's intentions. See also mm. 8, 15, and 33.

* Barber wrote *"cadenza"* under this measure in the violin part; his intention is unclear.

APPENDIX 1:
MANUSCRIPT FACSIMILE
Violin Part Only,
Sonata for Violin and Piano,
First Movement

Feb. 14, 1928

APPENDIX 2:
MANUSCRIPT FACSIMILE
Cover and Page One,
Gypsy Dance

GYPSY DANCE

from-
"The Rose Tree"

by

Samuel O. Barber. II.

Arranged for a

Violin Solo.

COVER DESIGNED BY WILLIAM. PALMER. LEAR.

ABOUT THE RECORDING ARTISTS

Violinist **Frank Almond** is Concertmaster of the Milwaukee Symphony Orchestra. He returned to the MSO after holding positions as Concertmaster of the Rotterdam Philharmonic with Valery Gergiev, and Guest Concertmaster of the London Philharmonic with Kurt Masur. He continues an active schedule of solo and chamber music performances in the U.S. and abroad including the Ojai Festival, the American String Project in Seattle, the Nara Academy in Nara, Japan, Jazz at Lincoln Center, Music in the Vineyards, Chamber Music Society of Lincoln Center, the Ravinia Festival, La Jolla Summerfest, and various solo appearances with orchestras. He has been a member of the chamber group An die Musik in New York City since 1997, and also directs the highly successful Frankly Music Chamber Series based in Milwaukee. At 17, he was one of the youngest prizewinners in the history of the Nicolò Paganini Competition in Genoa, Italy, and five years later was one of two American prizewinners at the Eighth International Tchaikovsky Competition in Moscow, which was documented in an award-winning PBS film. He has recorded for Summit, Albany, Boolean (his own label), Innova, Newport Classic, Wergo and New Albion, and has appeared numerous times on NPR's Performance Today. The re-release of Mr. Almond's recording of the complete Brahms Sonatas, performed in collaboration with pianist William Wolfram, brought extraordinary critical acclaim. *BBC Music Magazine* wrote, "...the disc ends with an explosive finale which reaffirms the players' unassailable technical mastery and absolute temperamental harmonization." A review from *American Record Guide* was equally enthusiastic: "...this is easily the greatest Brahms I have ever heard. Almond and Wolfram tower above giants." It was also listed in the *American Record Guide* top recordings. Frank's CD of Resphighi, Strauss and Janáek with William Wolfram on the AVIE label was named a "Best of 2007 by the *American Record Guide*. His CD of American violin and piano music was released on Innova Recordings with pianist Brian Zeger. He recorded the three volume set The Violin Collection for G. Schirmer/Hal Leonard. Mr. Almond holds two degrees from the Juilliard School, where he studied with Dorothy DeLay. Other important teachers included Michael Tseitlin, Felix Galimir, and Joseph Silverstein.

Frank Almond plays on a violin by Antonio Stradivari from 1715, the "ex-Lipniski." All selections on the CD were recorded in 2010 on this instrument except *Canzone*, which was recorded in 2006 on a 1624 violin made by Antonio and Hieronymus Amati.

Pianist **Laura Ward** maintains an active career as a performer and educator. As a founding director of Lyric Fest (www.lyricfest.org), she has developed in Philadelphia one of the most innovativevocal recital series in the U.S. Recent concert engagements have taken her to Carnegie Hall, the Kennedy Center, and Boston's Isabella Stewart Gardner Museum. She has performed at international music festivals such as the Spoleto Festival (Italy), the Colmar International Music Festival, and Saint Denis Festival in France. Ms. Ward has served as a vocal coach at The Academy of Vocal Arts, Westminster Choir College Temple University, Ravinia Festival Stean's Institute, Washington Opera, University of Maryland, Music Academy of the West, and at Cleveland's Blossom Festival. In addition, she is the official pianist for the Washington International Vocal Competition and the Marian Anderson Award. Ms. Ward has made dozens of recordings for Hal Leonard and G. Schirmer, and is the co-editor of *Gabriel Fauré: 50 Songs*, and *Johannes Brahms: 75 Songs*.

Pianist **Michael Mizrahi** has appeared as concerto soloist, recitalist, chamber musician, and music educator across the U.S. and Europe, and in Japan. He has performed as soloist with the Houston Symphony, National Symphony Orchestra, Sioux City Symphony, Prince Georges Philharmonic Orchestra, and The Haddonfield Symphony (now Symphony in C), and in such venues as Carnegie Hall, Philadelphia's Kimmel Center for the Performing Arts, The Kennedy Center, Boston's Jordan Hall, and Houston's Jones Hall. He has appeared in recital on Chicago's Dame Myra Hess Concert Series, Houston's Channing Recital Series, and at Washington, D.C's Phillips Collection. A recent fellow of The Academy: A Program of Carnegie Hall, the Juilliard School, and the Weill Music Institute (ACJW), he is a founding member of NOW Ensemble, which released its debut CD, *NOW*, in 2008 and recorded its second CD in the summer of 2010. He is also a founding member of the Moët Trio. Mr. Mizrahi is a winner of Astral Artists' 2005 National Auditions. He also captured First Prize and the Audience Choice Award in the Ima Hogg Competition, as well as first prizes in the National Symphony Orchestra's Young Soloists Competition, Berkeley Piano Club Competition, International Bartok-Kabalevsky Competition, and the Iowa International Piano Competition. His CD of 21st-century works for piano is on the New Amsterdam label. Michael Mizrahi holds a Doctor of Musical Arts degree from the Yale School of Music. He is Assistant Professor of Piano at the Lawrence University Conservatory of Music in Appleton, Wisconsin.

Born in Caracas, Venezuela, pianist **Elena Abend** has performed with all the major orchestras of her country and has recorded with the Filarmonica Nacional. As the recipient of a scholarship from the Venezuelan Council for the Arts, Ms. Abend studied at the Juilliard School, where she received her Bachelor and Master degrees. She has performed at the Purcell Room in London's Royal Festival Hall, Avery Fisher Hall in New York's Lincoln Center, Weill Recital Hall at Carnegie Hall and the Academy of Music with the Philadelphia Orchestra. Other engagements have included the Wigmore Hall in London, the Toulouse Conservatoire in France, the Corcoran Gallery in Washington D.C., the United Nations, Merkin Concert Hall in New York, Chicago Cultural Center, the Pabst Theater in Milwaukee, the Atlanta Historical Society, the Teresa Carreno Cultural Center in Caracas, as well as the Theatre Luxembourg in Meaux, France. Other chamber music collaborations include numerous performances at the Ravinia and Marlboro Music Festivals, as well as live broadcasts on Philadelphia's WFLN, The Dame Myra Hess Concert Series on Chicago's WFMT and Wisconsin Public Radio at the Elvehjem Museum in Madison, Wisconsin. Ms. Abend has recorded the three volume *Violin Collection* the three-volume *Clarinet Collection*, and the three-volume *Flute Collection* for G. Schirmer/Hal Leonard. A CD with clarinetist Todd Levy, performing the two Brahms Sonatas and the Schumann Fantasy and Romance pieces was released on the Avie label. She is editor and recording artist for two volumes of Mozart for piano in the Schirmer Performance Editions series. Ms. Abend is on the music faculty at the University of Wisconsin-Milwaukee.

ABOUT THE ENHANCED CDs

In addition to full performances and piano accompaniments playable on both your CD player and computer, these enhanced CDs also include tempo adjustment and transposition software for computer use only. This software, known as Amazing Slow Downer, was originally created for use in pop music to allow singers and players the freedom to independently adjust both tempo and pitch elements. Because we believe there may be valuable educational use for these features in classical and theatre music, we have included this software as a tool for both the teacher and student. For quick and easy installation instructions of this software, please see below.

In recording a piano accompaniment we necessarily must choose one tempo. Our choice of tempo, phrasing, *ritardandos*, and dynamics is carefully considered. But by the nature of recording, it is only one option.

However, we encourage you to explore your own interpretive ideas, which may differ from our recordings. This new software feature allows you to adjust the tempo up and down without affecting the pitch. Likewise, Amazing Slow Downer allows you to shift pitch up and down without affecting the tempo. We recommend that these new tempo and pitch adjustment features be used with care and insight. Ideally, you will be using these recorded accompaniments and Amazing Slow Downer for practice only.

The audio quality may be somewhat compromised when played through the Amazing Slow Downer. This compromise in quality will not be a factor in playing the CD audio track on a normal CD player or through another audio computer program.

INSTALLATION INSTRUCTIONS:

For Macintosh OS 8, 9 and X:
- Load the CD-ROM into your CD-ROM Drive on your computer.
- Each computer is set up a little differently. Your computer may automatically open the audio CD portion of this enhanced CD and begin to play it.
- To access the CD-ROM features, double-click on the data portion of the CD-ROM (which will have the Hal Leonard icon in red and be named as the book).
- Double-click on the "Amazing OS 8 (9 or X)" folder.
- Double-click "Amazing Slow Downer"/"Amazing OS X" to run the software from the CD-ROM, or copy this file to your hard disk and run it from there.
- Follow the instructions on-screen to get started. The Amazing Slow Downer should display tempo, pitch and mix bars. Click to select your track and adjust pitch or tempo by sliding the appropriate bar to the left or to the right.

For Windows:
- Load the CD-ROM into your CD-ROM Drive on your computer.
- Each computer is set up a little differently. Your computer may automatically open the audio CD portion of this enhanced CD and begin to play it.
- To access the CD-ROM features, click on My Computer then right click on the Drive that you placed the CD in. Click Open. You should then see a folder named "Amazing Slow Downer". Click to open the "Amazing Slow Downer" folder.
- Double-click "setup.exe" to install the software from the CD-ROM to your hard disk. Follow the on-screen instructions to complete installation.
- Go to "Start," "Programs" and find the "Amazing Slow Downer" folder. Go to that folder and select the "Amazing Slow Downer" software.
- Follow the instructions on-screen to get started. The Amazing Slow Downer should display tempo, pitch and mix bars. Click to select your track and adjust pitch or tempo by sliding the appropriate bar to the left or to the right.
- Note: On Windows NT, 2000, XP and Vista, the user should be logged in as the "Administrator" to guarantee access to the CD-ROM drive. Please see the help file for further information.

MINIMUM SYSTEM REQUIREMENTS:

For Macintosh:
Power Macintosh; Mac OS 8.5 or higher; 4 MB Application RAM; 8x Multi-Session CD-ROM drive

For Windows:
Pentium, Celeron or equivalent processor; Windows 95, 98, ME, NT, 2000, XP, Vista, Windows 7 ; 4 MB Application RAM; 8x Multi-Session CD-ROM drive